# Navigating Through Grace

by

Joshua Alvarez

# Navigating Through Grace

## by

## Joshua Alvarez

**Publishing Company**
Joshua Alvarez

*First Edition*

Copyright © 2016

ISBN-13: 978-0997308594 (Joshua A. Alvarez)

ISBN-10: 0997308591

**Unless otherwise noted, all Scripture quotations are from the New American Standard Version of the Bible.**

Scripture quotations taken from the New American Standard Bible®, Copyright © 1960, 1962, 1963, 1968, 1971, 1972, 1973, 1975, 1977, 1995 by The Lockman Foundation. Used by permission. (www.Lockman.org)

Scripture quotations taken from the Holy Bible, New International Version®, NIV® Copyright ©1973, 1978,

## *Dedication*

To my Lovely wife Alyssa for all the sacrifices that she makes. Without her, this book would not be possible. To my beautiful daughter Purity, whom the Lord has blessed me with to brighten my every day. To my mother-in-law, for her love and care of my daughter. Without her, our lives would be much more complicated. Lastly, to my precious Lord and Savior, Jesus Christ, to whom I rightfully owe my life and whom I fearfully serve, desperately need, and so dearly love.

# *Table of Contents*

## I. THE LENS OF LOVE:

1. It is imperative that we look at Scripture through the lens of love and with the intention of growing in love:

   a) *"But now __faith, hope, love, abide these three__; but the __greatest of these is love.__" – 1 Corinthians 13:13*

      - We should live in love.

2. Loving is the greatest commandment and the most important thing we do as believers:

   a) *"One of the scribes came and heard them arguing, and recognizing that He had answered them well, asked Him, '__What commandment is the foremost of all__?' Jesus answered, "__The foremost is__, 'HEAR, O ISRAEL! THE LORD OUR GOD IS ONE LORD; AND YOU SHALL __LOVE THE LORD YOUR GOD WITH ALL YOUR HEART__, AND WITH __ALL YOUR SOUL__, AND WITH __ALL YOUR MIND__, AND WITH __ALL YOUR STRENGTH.__" – Mark 12:28-30*

3. Understanding and **encountering God's love** for us **allows us to love God in a wholehearted way**:

   a) *"__We love, __because He first loved us__." – 1 John 4:19*

      - We love because we have encountered God's love.

   b) *"And __you will know the truth__, and __the truth will make you free__." – John 8:32*

      - Knowing the truth about God's love for us is paramount.

c) Encountering God's unconditional, perfect love, not only allows us to love God in a wholehearted way, but allows us to love ourselves and others.

4. The four spheres of love:

a) Understanding and encountering God's love for us. (All spheres of love are contingent upon this.)

b) Our love for God. (The remaining two spheres of love are contingent upon the first two.)

c) Our love for ourselves.

d) Our love for others.

5. Everything is about love:

a) *"On these two commandments **depend the whole Law** and the Prophets." – Matthew 22:40*

- Loving God, loving our neighbor, loving ourselves.

6. If everything is about love, then we should read the Word of God with the mindset of growing in the four spheres of love:

a) *"If you keep My commandments, **you will abide in My love**; just as I have kept My Father's commandments and abide in His love." – John 15:10*

- God gives us His Word to teach us how to live in His love.

7. **Love is the desire of God's heart:**

a) *"But go and learn what this means: '**I DESIRE COMPASSION.**'" – Matthew 9:13*

8. The sacrifice and effort that we put into our relationship with God was meant to position us to grow in the four spheres of love. <u>Sacrifice in itself is not the end product</u>:

  a) *"But go and learn what this means: **'I DESIRE COMPASSION, AND NOT SACRIFICE,**' for I did not come to call the righteous, but sinners." – Matthew 9:13*

   - The Old Testament reference Hosea 6:6 can be translated as "I desire covenant love."

   - It is love that God desires from us.

9. Love is the very essence of who God is:

  a) *"The one who does not love does not know God, for **God is love**." – 1 John 4:8*

10. Satan wants to prevent our knowledge of who God is, including our knowledge of God's love:

  a) *"<u>We are destroying speculations and **every lofty thing raised up against the knowledge of God**</u>, and we are taking every thought captive to the obedience of Christ." – 2 Corinthians 10:5*

11. <u>Sound Doctrine (sound teaching) is vital to our spiritual growth</u>. **Spiritual growth is growing in the four spheres of love**:

  a) *"**<u>All Scripture</u>** is **<u>inspired by God</u>** and **<u>profitable for teaching</u>**, for **<u>reproof</u>**, for **<u>correction</u>**, for **<u>training in righteousness</u>**." – 2 Timothy 3:16*

b) *"For the time will come **when they will not endure sound doctrine**; but wanting to have their ears tickled, they will accumulate for themselves teachers in accordance to their own desires." – 2 Timothy 4:3*

c) *"**But we know that the Law is good, if one uses it lawfully**, realizing the fact that law is not made for a righteous person, but for those who are lawless and rebellious, for the ungodly and sinners, for the unholy and profane, for those who kill their fathers or mothers, for murderers and immoral men and homosexuals and kidnappers and liars and perjurers, and **whatever else is contrary to sound teaching**." – 1 Timothy 1:8-10*

- The law is not meant to incriminate believers. The law is good, if we use it to grow in love.

d) *"**If you keep My commandments, you will abide in My love**; just as I have kept My Father's commandments and abide in His love." – John 15:10*

e) *"He **who has My commandments and keeps them is the one who loves Me**; and he who loves Me will be loved by My Father, **and I will love him and will disclose Myself to him**." – John 14:21*

- When we keep God's commandments, God will love our obedience and will reveal Himself to a greater degree, which in turn will cause us to love Him more.

f) *"Woe to you, scribes and Pharisees, hypocrites! <u>For you tithe mint and dill and cummin,</u> and <u>have</u> **<u>neglected the weightier provisions of the law</u>**: **<u>justice</u>** and **<u>mercy</u>** and **<u>faithfulness</u>**; but these are the things you should have done without neglecting the others. You blind guides, **<u>who strain out a gnat and swallow a camel</u>**!"* – Matthew 23:23-24

- Justice, mercy, and faithfulness are all acts of love.

g) *"<u>And you will know the truth, and the truth will make you free.</u>"* – John 8:32

h) *"**<u>You search the Scriptures</u>** because you think that in them you have eternal life; **<u>it is these that testify about Me</u>**; and <u>you are unwilling to come to Me so that you may have life.</u> I do not receive glory from men; <u>but I know you, that **you do not have the love of God in yourselves**</u>."* – John 5:39-42

- The factual knowledge of Scripture in themselves do not give life, but point us to Jesus who gives life. Factual knowledge must produce intimate knowledge of Jesus.

i) *"Therefore **the Law has become our tutor to lead us to Christ**, so that we may be justified by faith."* – Galatians 3:24

j) *"That <u>He would grant you, according to the riches of His glory,</u> to be strengthened with power through His Spirit in the inner man, so that Christ may dwell in your hearts through faith; and that you, <u>being</u>*

*rooted and grounded in love, may be able to comprehend* with all the saints what is the **breadth** and **length** and **height** and **depth,** and **to know the love of Christ which surpasses knowledge, that you may be filled up to all the fullness of God.**" – *Ephesians 3:16-19*

- Growing in knowledge of God's love and in the actions of God's love is true spiritual growth.

## II. THE KNOWLEDGE OF GOD:

1. The believer is capable of knowing God:

   a) *"And may be found in Him, not having a righteousness of my own derived from the Law, but that which is through faith in Christ, the righteousness which comes from God on the basis of faith, **that I may know Him** and the power of His resurrection and the fellowship of His sufferings, being conformed to His death."* – Philippians 3:9-10

   b) *"But we all, **with unveiled face, beholding as in a mirror the glory of the Lord**, are being transformed into the same image from glory to glory, just as from the Lord, the Spirit."* – 2 Corinthians 3:18

   c) *"And the disciples came and said to Him, '**Why do You speak to them in parables**?' Jesus answered them, '**To you it has been granted to know the mysteries of the kingdom of heaven**, but to them it has not been granted. For whoever has, to him more shall be given, and he will have an abundance; but whoever does not have, even what he has shall be taken away from him. Therefore I speak to them in parables; because **while seeing they do not see**, and **while hearing they do not hear, nor do they understand**."* – Matthew 13:10-13

   d) *"**He made known His ways to Moses**, His acts to the sons of Israel."* – Psalms 103:7

2.  We can know God with clarity:

a)  *"So that you may **know the exact truth** about the things you have been taught."* – Luke 1:4

b)  *"This man had been instructed in the way of the Lord; and being fervent in spirit, **he was speaking and teaching accurately the things concerning Jesus**, being acquainted only with the baptism of John."* – Acts 18:25

c)  *"That their hearts may be encouraged, having been knit together in love, and attaining to all the wealth that comes **from the full assurance of understanding**, resulting in a true knowledge of God's mystery, that is, Christ Himself."* – Colossians 2:2

d)  *"Let us draw near with a sincere heart in **full assurance of faith**, having our hearts sprinkled clean from an evil conscience and our bodies washed with pure water."* – Hebrews 10:22

e)  *"And we desire that each one of you show the same diligence so **as to realize the full assurance of hope** until the end."* – Hebrews 6:11

f)  *"Epaphras, who is one of your number, a bondslave of Jesus Christ, sends you his greetings, always laboring earnestly for you in his prayers, that you may stand perfect and **fully assured in all the will of God**."* – Colossians 4:12

g)  *"And do not be conformed to this world, but be transformed by the renewing of your mind, **so that*** *you may prove what the will of God is, that which is **good** and **acceptable** and **perfect**." – Romans 12:2*

h) *"Walk as children of Light (for the fruit of the Light consists in all goodness and righteousness and truth), **trying to learn what is pleasing to the Lord.**"* – Ephesians 5:8-10

- Put effort into learning what pleases God.

3. The source of truth is God, so knowing truth is knowing God:

a) *"But **the Helper, the Holy Spirit, whom the Father will send in My name, He will teach you all things**, and bring to your remembrance all that I said to you." – John 14:26*

b) *"For this reason also, since the day we heard of it, we have not ceased to pray for you and to ask that you may **be filled with the knowledge of His will in all spiritual wisdom and understanding**, so that you will walk in a manner worthy of the Lord, to please Him in all respects, bearing fruit in every good work and **increasing in the knowledge of God**." – Colossians 1:9-10*

c) *"But **grow in the grace and knowledge of our Lord and Savior Jesus Christ.** To Him be the glory, both now and to the day of eternity. Amen." – 2 Peter 3:18*

d) *"Seeing that His divine power has granted to us everything pertaining to life and godliness, **through*** *the true knowledge of Him* who called us by His own glory and excellence." – 2 Peter 1:3

e)   "The ostriches' wings flap joyously with the pinion and plumage of love, for she abandons her eggs to the earth and warms them in the dust, and **she forgets** that a foot may crush them, or that a wild beast may trample them. She treats her young cruelly, as if they were not hers; though her labor be in vain, she is unconcerned; **Because God has made her forget wisdom, and has not given her a share of understanding**." – Job 39:13-17

f)   "But if any of you lacks wisdom, **let him ask of God, who gives to all generously and without reproach, and it will be given to him**." – James 1:5

## III. GROWING IN OUR KNOWLEDGE OF GOD:

1.  Consistency and relentless perseverance over time is necessary to grow in the knowledge of God:

    a)  *"So Jesus was saying to those Jews who had believed Him, '__If you continue in My word__, then you are truly disciples of Mine; __and you will know the truth__, and the truth will make you free.'" – John 8:31-32*

    b)  *"__If you seek her as silver and search for her as for hidden treasures; then you will discern the fear of the LORD and discover the knowledge of God__." – Proverbs 2:4-5*

    c)  *"__Keep on asking__, and you will receive what you ask for. Keep on seeking, and you will find. Keep on knocking, and the door will be opened to you." – Matthew 7:7, NLT*

2.  Growing in the knowledge of God requires hunger and effort:

    a)  *"Blessed are those __who hunger and thirst for righteousness, for they shall be satisfied__." – Matthew 5:6*

    b)  *"Then he said to me, "Do not be afraid, <u>Daniel</u>, __for from the first day that you set your heart on understanding__ <u>this and on humbling yourself before your God, your words were heard, and I have come in response to your words.</u>" – Daniel 10:12*

c) *"Now on the last day, the great day of the feast, Jesus stood and cried out, saying, "If anyone is thirsty, **let him come** to Me and drink."* – John 7:37

d) *"He who has My commandments and keeps them is the one who loves Me; and **he who loves Me** will be loved by My Father, and **I will love him and will disclose Myself to him**."* – John 14:21

e) *" **If you seek** her (truth, understanding) **as silver and search for her as for hidden treasures; then** you will discern the fear of the LORD and discover the knowledge of God."* – Proverbs 2:4-5

3. Purity is necessary to grow in the knowledge of God:

a) *"Blessed are the **pure in heart, for they shall see God**."* – Matthew 5:8

b) *"Pursue peace with all men, and **the sanctification without which no one will see the Lord**."* – Hebrews 12:14

c) *"Then Moses said to Aaron, "It is what the LORD spoke, saying, **'By those who come near Me I will be treated as holy**, And before all the people I will be honored.' So Aaron, therefore, kept silent."* – Leviticus 10:3

d) *"You must warn each other every day, while it is still "today," so that none of you will **be deceived by sin and hardened against God**."* – Hebrews 3:13, NLT

e) *"That, in reference to your former manner of life, you lay aside the old self, which is being corrupted in* accordance with the **lusts of deceit.**" – *Ephesians 4:22*

f) "**For sin**, *taking an opportunity through the commandment,* **deceived me** *and through it killed me.*" – *Romans 7:11*

g) "**For the LORD gives wisdom**; *from His mouth come knowledge and understanding.* **He stores up sound wisdom for the upright**; *He is a shield to those who walk in integrity.*" – *Proverbs 2:6-7*

4. **Faith**, **obedience**, **wholeheartedness** and a **revelation of the beauty of Jesus**:

a) "**The kingdom of heaven is like a treasure hidden in the field**, *which a man found and hid again; and* **from joy over it** *he goes and* **sells all that he has and buys that field.**" – *Matthew 13:44*

b) "**You will seek Me and find Me when you search for Me with all your heart**." – *Jeremiah 29:13*

c) "**if you will receive my words** *and treasure my commandments within you...then you will discern the fear of the LORD and discover the knowledge of God.*" – *Proverbs 2:1,5*

d) "*Therefore* **everyone who hears these words of Mine and acts on them**, *may be* **compared to a wise man** *who built his house on the rock. And the rain fell, and the floods came, and the winds blew and slammed against that house; and yet it did not fall, for it had been founded on the rock.*" – *Matthew 7:24-25*

13

e) *"And those are the ones on <u>whom seed was sown on the good soil</u>; and **they hear the word and accept it** and **bear fruit**, <u>thirty, sixty, and a hundredfold."</u>* – Mark 4:20

f) *"But **prove yourselves doers of the word, and not merely hearers** who **delude** themselves." – James 1:22*

5. Growing in the knowledge of God requires that we fill our heart and mind with truth:

a) *"My Son **if...Make your ear attentive to wisdom, Incline your heart to understanding...Then you will discern the fear of the LORD and discover the knowledge of God**." – Proverbs 2:1, 2, 5*

b) *"And do not be conformed to this world, <u>but be transformed by the renewing of your mind, so that you may prove what the will of God is, that which is good and acceptable and perfect</u>." – Romans 12:2*

c) *"**Be diligent to present yourself approved to God** as a workman who does not need to be ashamed, **accurately handling the word of truth**." – 2 Timothy 2:15*

d) *"**But his delight is in the law of the LORD, and in His law he meditates day and night**. <u>He will be like a tree firmly planted by streams of water which yields its fruit in its season and its leaf does not wither; and in whatever he does, he prospers.</u>" – Psalms 1:2-3*

e) *"But He answered and said, "It is written, <u>'MAN SHALL NOT LIVE ON BREAD ALONE, BUT **ON EVERY WORD THAT PROCEEDS OUT OF THE MOUTH OF GOD.**'"</u> – Matthew 4:4*

f) *"And <u>that from childhood **you have known the sacred writings which are able to give you the wisdom**</u> <u>that leads to salvation through faith which is in Christ Jesus."</u> – 2 Timothy 3:15*

6. Asking to acquire the knowledge of God:

a) *"You lust and do not have; so you commit murder. You are envious and cannot obtain; so you fight and quarrel. **You do not have because you do not ask.**" – James 4:2*

b) *"**You ask and do not receive**, <u>because you ask with wrong motives, so that you may spend it on your pleasures."</u> – James 4:3*

c) *"This is the confidence which we have before Him, that, <u>if we ask anything **according to His will**, He hears us."</u> – 1 John 5:14*

d) *"But <u>if any of you **lacks wisdom, let him ask of God, who gives to all generously and without reproach, and it will be given to him**</u>." – James 1:5*

e) *"For <u>if you cry for discernment, **Lift your voice for understanding**...Then you will discern the fear of the LORD and discover the knowledge of God."</u> – Proverbs 2:3,5*

7. Growing in the knowledge of God requires apostolic teaching:

a) "***They were continually devoting themselves to the apostles' teaching*** *and to fellowship, to the breaking of bread and to prayer.*" Acts 2:42

b) "*forsaking the right way, they have gone astray,* ***having followed the way of Balaam****, the son of Beor, who loved the wages of unrighteousness;*" 2 Peter 2:15

c) "*Yet this you do have**, that you hate the deeds of the Nicolaitans**, which I also hate.*" Revelations 2:6

d) "*So you also have some who in the same way **hold the teaching of the Nicolaitans.** Therefore repent; or else I am coming to you quickly, and I will make war against them with the sword of My mouth.*" Revelation 2:15-16

e) "*But I have a few things against you, **because you have there some who hold the teaching of Balaam, who kept teaching Balak** to put a stumbling block before the sons of Israel, to eat things sacrificed to idols and to commit acts of immorality.*" Revelation 2:14

f) "*But I have this against you**, that you tolerate** the woman Jezebel, who calls herself a prophetess, and **she teaches and leads My bond-servants astray** so that they commit acts of immorality and eat things sacrificed to idols.*" Revelations 2:20

16

g) *"Behold, <u>I will cause those of the</u> **synagogue of Satan**, who say that they are Jews and are not, but lie-- I will make them come and bow down at your feet, and make them know that I have loved you."* Revelation 3:9

h) *"For the time will come when **they will not endure sound doctrine**; <u>but wanting to have their ears tickled,</u> **they will accumulate for themselves teachers in accordance to their own desires**,"* 2 Timothy 4:3

i) *"preach the word; be ready in season and out of season; <u>reprove, rebuke, exhort, with great patience and instruction.</u>"* 2 Timothy 4:2

j) *"**All Scripture** is **inspired** by God and **profitable for teaching**, for **reproof**, for **correction**, for **training in righteousness**; so that the man of God may be adequate, **equipped for every good work**."* 2 Timothy 3:16-17

k) *"**My people are destroyed for lack of knowledge**. Because you have rejected knowledge, I also will reject you from being My priest. Since you have forgotten the law of your God, I also will forget your children."* Hosea 4:6

## IV. RIGHTEOUSNESS:

1. **Justification (no participation)** - (legal position) what we freely receive in the Spirit **by faith in Jesus Christ**.

   a) *"For we maintain that a man is justified by faith apart from works of the Law." – Romans 3:28*

2. **Sanctification (requires active participation)** - (living condition) is how much we actually experience of that which is freely available.

   b) *"Present your members as slaves to righteousness, resulting in sanctification." – Romans 6:19*

## V. PREVALENT TEACHINGS OF SANCTIFICATION:

1. **Instant Sanctification:** Teaching that salvation is <u>limited</u> to instant sanctification.

---

**Initial Sanctification:** Salvation <u>is not limited to</u> our initial sanctification when receiving Christ, but <u>does include</u> an initial sanctification.

a) *"But you <u>were</u> washed, but you <u>were</u> sanctified, but you were justified in the name of the Lord Jesus, and in the Spirit of our God." – 1 Corinthians 6:11*

b) *"If anyone is in Christ, he is a new creature; the old things passed away; behold, <u>new things have come</u>." – 2 Corinthians 5:17*

   - We are both completely transformed and being transformed.

c) *"But we all, with unveiled face, beholding as in a mirror the glory of the Lord, **<u>are being transformed</u>** <u>into the same image from glory to glory</u>, just as from the Lord, the Spirit." – 2 Corinthians 3:18*

---

2. **Passive Sanctification:** Teaching that we play no part in the sanctification process.

---

**Sanctification Is a Continuous Process:** Sanctification is a continuous process in which we actively participate.

a) *"**Present** your members as slaves to righteousness, resulting in sanctification." – Romans 6:19*

b) *"He (John the Baptist) was the lamp that was burning and was shining and you were willing to rejoice **for a while** in his light." – John 5:35*

c) *"And **working together with Him**, we also urge you not to receive the grace of God in vain." – 2 Corinthians 6:1*

d) "Therefore, brethren, **be all the more diligent** to make certain about His calling and choosing you; **for as long as you practice these things, you will never stumble**." – 2 Peter 1:10

---

3.  **Perfect sanctification:** Teaching that we are already perfect and sinless **in *our living condition*.**

---

Although **we are perfectly righteous in our legal position before God,** in our living condition we are still growing.

a)  *"For I am confident of this very thing, that He who **began a good work** in you **will perfect it** until the day of Christ Jesus."* – Philippians 1:6

b)  *"The LORD **will accomplish what concerns me**; Your lovingkindness, O LORD, is everlasting; **Do not forsake the works of Your hands.**"* – Psalms 138:8

c)  *"For we are **God's masterpiece**. He has created us anew in Christ Jesus, so we can do the good things he planned for us long ago."* – Ephesians 2:10, NLT

d)  *"Therefore, my dear friends, as you have always obeyed--not only in my presence, but now much more in my absence-- **continue to work out your salvation** with fear and trembling."* – Philippians 2:12, NIV

---

## VI. SALVATION IS A THREE PART PROCESS: JUSTIFICATION, SANCTIFICATION, AND GLORIFICATION:

1. **JUSTIFICATION:**

   - Definition: to declared legally righteous.

   - Application: Victory over penalty of sin.

   a) We have been **justified**:

   1) *"Having been **justified** by faith, we have peace with God through our Lord Jesus Christ." – Romans 5:1*

   b) We are saved by **grace** through **faith** in Jesus Christ:

   1) *"For **by grace** you have been saved through **faith**; and that not of yourselves, it is the **gift of God**." – Ephesians 2:8*

   2) *"Who are protected by the power of God **through faith** for a salvation ready to be revealed in the last time." – 1 Peter 1:5*

   3) *"Because God has chosen you from the beginning for salvation through sanctification by the Spirit and **faith in the truth**." – 2 Thessalonians 2:13*

2. **SANCTIFICATION:**

   - Definition: to be set apart for a holy use.

   - Application: Victory over bondage of sin.

   a) We have experienced an initial sanctification and are currently being sanctified:

1) *"You were washed, but you were Sanctified, but you were Justified **in the name of the Lord Jesus Christ** and in the Spirit of our God." – 1 Corinthians 6:11*

2) *"For by that one offering he forever made perfect those who are being made holy." – Hebrews 10:14, NLT*

b) "His great instrument of cleansing is '**the Word**' in all its: searching, humbling, rebuking, correcting, informing, stimulating, refreshing, and consoling power."[1] – Pulpit Commentary

1) *"Christ also loved the church and gave Himself up for her, so that He might sanctify her, having cleansed her by the washing of water with the word." – Ephesians 5:25-26*

2) *"Sanctify them in the truth; Your word is truth." – John 17:17*

3) *"You are already clean because of the word which I have spoken to you." – John 15:3*

c) The **Holy Spirit** has a role in the sanctification process:

1) *"Because God has chosen you from the beginning for **salvation** through **sanctification by the Spirit** and **faith in the truth**." – 2 Thessalonians 2:13*

2) *"By the sanctifying work of the Spirit" – 1 Peter 1:2*

---

[1] BibleSoft Inc., *The Pulpit Commentary: Electronic Database* (Bible Soft, 2001-2010), accessed through
http://biblehub.com/commentaries/pulpit/ephesians/5.htm

d) The role **obedience** has in the <u>sanctification process</u>:

1) *"Since you have <u>in **obedience to the truth** purified</u> <u>your souls</u> for a sincere love of the brethren, fervently love one another from the heart."* – 1 Peter 1:22

2) *"Through whom we have received grace and apostleship <u>to bring about **the obedience of faith**</u>"* – Romans 1:5

3) *"But **<u>if we walk in the Light</u>** <u>as He Himself is in the Light</u>, we have fellowship with one another, **<u>and</u>** <u>the blood of Jesus His Son</u> **<u>cleanses us from all sin</u>**."* – 1 John 1:7

4) *"So then, my beloved, <u>just as you have always obeyed</u>, not as in my presence only, but now much more in my absence, **work out** <u>your salvation with fear and trembling</u>."* – Philippians 2:12

5) *"And having been made perfect, **He became to all those who obey Him the source of eternal salvation**."* – Hebrews 5:9

3. **GLORIFICATION:**

- Definition: is the future and final work of God upon Christians where he transforms our mortal physical bodies to the eternal physical bodies in which we will dwell forever.

- Application: redemption of the body and from the sin nature.

a) We will be Glorified:

1) Receive **Resurrected Glorified Bodies:**

A. *"The **resurrection** of the dead. It is sown a perishable body, it is **raised** an **imperishable body**; it is sown in dishonor, it is **raised in glory**; it is sown in weakness, it is **raised in power**; it is sown a natural body, it is **raised a spiritual body**. If there is a natural body, there is also a **spiritual body**...Behold, I tell you a mystery; we will not all sleep, but we will all be changed...the dead will be **raised imperishable**, and we will be changed. For this perishable must put on the **imperishable**, and this mortal must **put on immortality**." – 1 Corinthians 15:42-44,51-53*

2) Christ glorified body:

A. *"**See My (Jesus)** hands and My feet, that it is I Myself; touch Me and see, for **a spirit does not have flesh and bones as you see that I have.**" – Luke 24:39*

3) Our body will be **like Christ** resurrected body:

A. *"Who will transform the body of our humble state **into conformity with the body of His glory,** by the exertion of the power that He has even to subject all things to Himself." – Philippians 3:21*

B. *"When Christ, who is our life, is revealed, **then you also will be revealed with Him in glory."** Colossians 3:4*

C. *"Beloved, now we are children of God, and it has not appeared as yet what we will be. We know that when He appears, **we will be like Him**, because we will see Him just as He is." – 1 John 3:2*

D. *"For they cannot even die anymore, because **they are like angels**, and are sons of God, **being sons of the resurrection**." — Luke 20:36*

4) Our bodies will be **redeemed**:

A. *"For I consider that the sufferings of this present time are <u>not worthy to be compared with the **glory that is to be revealed to us**</u>. For the anxious longing of the <u>creation waits eagerly for the **revealing of the sons of God.**</u> And not only this, but also we ourselves, having the first fruits of the Spirit, even we ourselves groan within ourselves, <u>waiting eagerly for our adoption as sons, **the redemption of our body**</u>." — Romans 8:18-19, 23*

**VII. SANCTIFICATION, OUR LIVING CONDITION:**

**1. WORKS AND SAVING FAITH:**

a) Works DO NOT earn our salvation (we are saved by faith), yet **works TESTIFY** that we **TRULY** have a **SAVING FAITH**:

   1) *"What use is it, my brethren, if someone **says** he **has faith** but he **has no works? Can that faith save him?**...Even so **faith**, if it has no works, **is dead, being by itself.**"* – James 2:14, 17

   2) *"You believe that God is one. You do well; the demons also believe, and shudder. But **are you willing to recognize, you foolish fellow**, that faith without works is useless?"* – James 2:19-20

b) Faith **works together** with our works:

   1) *"You see that **faith was working with his works**, and as a result of the works, **faith was perfected**; and the Scripture was fulfilled which says, 'AND ABRAHAM BELIEVED GOD, AND IT WAS RECKONED TO HIM AS RIGHTEOUSNESS,' and he was called the friend of God. You see that a man is justified by works and **not by faith alone.**"* – James 2:22-24

**2. EFFORT:**

a) Putting effort into our relationship with Jesus is not legalism, the Lord expects, commands, and empowers us to put effort into our relationship with Him:

1) *"One of the scribes came and heard them arguing, and recognizing that He had answered them well, asked Him, 'What commandment is the foremost of all?' **Jesus answered, 'The foremost is**, 'HEAR, O ISRAEL! THE LORD OUR GOD IS ONE LORD; AND **YOU SHALL** LOVE THE LORD YOUR GOD WITH ALL YOUR HEART, AND WITH ALL YOUR SOUL, AND WITH ALL YOUR MIND, **AND WITH ALL YOUR STRENGTH.'"* – Mark 12:28-30*

2) *"**Strive** (make every effort) to enter through the narrow door; for many, I tell you, will seek to enter and will not be able."* – Luke 13:24, *(emphasis added)*

3) *"So then, my beloved, just as you have always obeyed, not as in my presence only, but now much more in my absence, **work out** your salvation with fear and trembling."* – Philippians 2:12

4) *"**Be diligent** to present yourself approved to God as a workman who does not need to be ashamed, accurately handling the word of truth."* – 2 Timothy 2:15

5) *"Therefore, brethren, be **all the more diligent** to make certain about His calling and choosing you; for as long as you practice these things, you will never stumble."* – 2 Peter 1:10

6) *"Therefore, beloved, since you look for these things, **be diligent** to be found by Him in peace, spotless and blameless."* – 2 Peter 3:14

7) *"That I may know Him and the power of His resurrection and the fellowship of His sufferings, being conformed to His death;* **in order** *that I may attain to the resurrection from the dead. Not that I have already obtained it or have already become perfect,* **but I press on** *so that I may lay hold of that for which also I was laid hold of by Christ Jesus." – Philippians 3:10-12*

8) *"By his divine power, God has given us everything we need for living a godly life. We have received all of this by coming to know him, the one who called us to himself by means of his marvelous glory and excellence." – 2 Peter 1:3, NLT*

## 3. WHOLEHEARTEDNESS:

A. God requires WHOLEHEARTEDNESS: Wholeheartedness is not to be confused with perfect maturity which we have not received in this state of being:

1) *"That I may know Him and the power of His resurrection and the fellowship of His sufferings, being conformed to His death; in order that I may attain to the resurrection from the dead.* **Not that I have already obtained it** *or have* **already become perfect,** *but* **I press on** *so that I may lay hold of that for which also I was laid hold of by Christ Jesus." – Philippians 3:10-12*

2) *"One of the scribes came and heard them arguing, and recognizing that He had answered them well, asked Him, 'What commandment is the* **foremost of all***?'* **Jesus answered, 'The***

*foremost is, 'HEAR, O ISRAEL! THE LORD OUR GOD IS ONE LORD; AND **YOU SHALL LOVE** THE LORD YOUR GOD **WITH ALL YOUR HEART**, AND WITH ALL YOUR SOUL, AND WITH ALL YOUR MIND, AND WITH ALL YOUR STRENGTH.'" – Mark 12:28-30*

3) *"**No one** can serve two masters; for either he will **hate the one** and **love the other**, or he will be **devoted to one** and **despise the other**. You cannot serve God and wealth." – Matthew 6:24*

4) *"Elijah came near to all the people and said, "How long will you **hesitate between two opinions**? If the LORD is God, **follow Him**; but if Baal, follow him." But the people did not answer him a word." – 1 Kings 18:21*

- Indecision is a decision.

5) *"You will seek Me and find Me **when** you search for Me **with all your heart**." – Jeremiah 29:13*

6) *"I will give them a heart to know Me, for I am the LORD; and they will be My people, and I will be their God, for they will return to Me **with their whole heart**." – Jeremiah 24:7*

7) *"As for you, my son Solomon, know the God of your father, and **serve Him with a whole heart** and a willing mind; for the LORD searches all hearts, and understands every intent of the thoughts. If you seek Him, He will let you find*

*Him; but if you forsake Him, He will reject you forever." – 1 Chronicles 28:9*

8) *"You adulteresses, do you not know that <u>friendship with the world</u> (the sinful things of this world) **is hostility toward God**? Therefore <u>whoever wishes to be a friend of the world makes himself an **enemy of God**.</u>" – James 4:4, (emphasis added)*

9) *"And they overcame him because of the blood of the Lamb and because of the word of their testimony, and <u>they did not love their life</u> (our lives outside of Christ) <u>even when faced with death.</u>" – Revelations 12:11, (emphasis added)*

10) *"<u>He who loves his life</u> (our lives outside of Christ) <u>loses it</u>, and <u>he who hates his life</u> (our lives outside of Christ) <u>in this world **will keep it to life eternal**.</u>" – John 12:25, (emphasis added)*

11) *"**After He** (God) had removed him (Saul), He raised up David to be their king, concerning whom **He also testified and said**, 'I have found David the son of Jesse, <u>a man after my heart, who will do **all My will**.</u>'" – Acts 13:22 (emphasis added)*

B. <u>A heart set on 100% OBEDIENCE</u> and <u>a heart set (goal) to be LIKE CHRIST</u>. A heart set to obey 100% does not imply perfection or a 100% success rate, nor does a goal to be like Christ imply a perfect reflection, but a notable reflection:

2) Christ obedience:

   a) *"Although He (Jesus) was a Son, **He learned obedience** from the things which He suffered"* – *Hebrews 5:8*

- Christ is our goal and our perfect example, the full expression of God.

   b) *"Being found in appearance as a man, He humbled Himself by becoming **obedient to the point of death**, even death on a cross."* – *Philippians 2:8*

   c) *"And He (Jesus) went down with them and came to Nazareth, and **He continued in subjection to them** (His parents)."* – *Luke 2:51 (emphasis added)*

   d) *"If you keep My commandments, you will abide in My love; just as **I (Jesus) have kept My Father's commandments** and abide in His love."* – *John 15:10 (emphasis added)*

   e) *"The Son is the radiance of God's glory and the exact representation of His being."* – *Hebrews 1:3, NIV*

C. A heart set to be like Christ (GOAL: Aim, ambition):

1) *"Therefore you are to be perfect, as your heavenly Father is perfect."* – *Matthew 5:48*

- Note: Make being like Jesus your aim or goal, specifically the way Jesus loved. When we love (love as defined by God) it is without fault.

2) *"Those who say they live in God <u>should live their lives as Jesus did.</u>"* – 1 John 2:6, NLT
3) *"Paul, an apostle of Christ Jesus according to the commandment of God our Savior, and of <u>Christ Jesus, **who is our hope**</u>."* – 1 Timothy 1:1

   - Jesus is our hope in many ways, including who we have set our hearts to be.

4) *"To them God has chosen to make known among the Gentiles the glorious riches of <u>this mystery, which is **Christ in you, the hope of Glory.**</u>"* – Colossians 1:27, NIV

   - Those who set their hearts to abide in Christ in this age will see the full manifestation in the next.

D. Our obedience:
   1) *"After He (God) had removed him (Saul), He raised up David to be their king, concerning whom <u>He also testified and said</u>, 'I have found David the son of Jesse, <u>a man after my heart, **who will do all My will.**</u>'"* – Acts 13:22, (emphasis added)

   2) *"For you have been called for this purpose, since Christ also suffered for you, <u>leaving you an example **for you to follow in His steps**</u>."* – 1 Peter 2:21

   3) *"<u>Be imitators of me, just as I also am of Christ.</u>"* – 1 Corinthians 11:1

   4) *"We are destroying speculations and every lofty thing raised up against the knowledge of God, and <u>we are taking every thought captive to the **obedience of Christ**</u>."* – 2 Corinthians 10:5

5) *"**And we are ready** to punish all disobedience, whenever your obedience is complete." – 2 Corinthians 10:6*

E. Our approach to **rebellion**, **disobedience**, and **lawlessness**:

1) *"**And we are ready** to punish all disobedience, whenever your obedience is complete." – 2 Corinthians 10:6*

F. What is lawlessness:

1) *"Everyone who **practices** sin also **practices lawlessness**; and sin is lawlessness." – 1 John 3:4*

G. Our former self:

1) *"**In which you formerly walked** according to the course of this world, according to the prince of the power of the air, of the spirit that is now working in the **sons of disobedience.**" – Ephesians 2:2*

2) *"For just as you presented your members as slaves to impurity and to lawlessness, **resulting in further lawlessness, so now** present your members as slaves to righteousness, resulting in sanctification." – Romans 6:19*

3) *"Therefore, putting aside all filthiness and all that remains of wickedness, in humility receive the word implanted, which is able to save your souls." – James 1:21*

4) *"that, in reference to **your former manner of life**, you lay aside the old self, which is being corrupted in*

*accordance with the lusts of deceit." – Ephesians 4:22*

5) *"Do not lie to one another, since **you laid aside the old self with its evil practices.**" – Colossians 3:9*

H. The spirit of rebellion:

1) *"**In which you formerly walked** according to the course of this world, according to the prince of the power of the air, of the <u>spirit that is</u> <u>now working</u> in the **sons of disobedience.**" – Ephesians 2:2*

I. New relationship with Christ inevitably means a new relationship with sin:

1) *"Do not be bound together with unbelievers<u>; for</u> <u>what partnership have righteousness and</u> <u>lawlessness, or</u> <u>what fellowship has light with</u> <u>darkness</u>?" – 2 Corinthians 6:14*

2) *"YOU HAVE LOVED RIGHTEOUSNESS **AND HATED LAWLESSNESS**; THEREFORE GOD, YOUR GOD, HAS ANOINTED YOU WITH THE OIL OF GLADNESS ABOVE YOUR COMPANIONS." – Hebrews 1:9*

- *Speaking of Jesus.*

3) *"Or do you not know that **your body is a temple of the Holy Spirit who is in you**, whom you have from God, and that you are not your own?" – 1 Corinthians 6:19*

J. Inward rebellion:

1) *"So you, too, outwardly appear righteous to men, but inwardly you are full of hypocrisy and lawlessness." – Matthew 23:28*

K. <u>We have been redeemed from lawlessness:</u>

1) *"<u>Who gave Himself (Jesus) for us **to redeem us** from **every lawless deed**</u>, and to purify for Himself a people for His own possession, zealous for good deeds." – Titus 2:14 (emphasis added)*

L. Lawlessness in the last days:

1) *"<u>Because lawlessness is increased</u>, most people's love will grow cold." – Matthew 24:12*

- In the last days (v. 3).

2) *"Let no one in any way deceive you, <u>for it will not come unless the **apostasy comes first**</u>, and <u>the man of lawlessness (Satan) is revealed</u>, the son of destruction." – 2 Thessalonians 2:3 (emphasis added)*

M. The penalty and righteous judgment on lawlessness:

1) *"Let no one deceive you with empty words, for because of these things the <u>wrath of God comes on the sons of disobedience</u>." – Ephesians 5:6*

2) *"And then I will declare to them, 'I never knew you; <u>DEPART FROM ME, **YOU WHO PRACTICE LAWLESSNESS.**</u>'" – Matthew 7:23*

3) *"The Son of Man will send forth His angels, and they will gather out of His kingdom all stumbling blocks,*

and those who commit lawlessness, and will throw them into the furnace of fire; in that place there will be weeping and gnashing of teeth." – Matthew 13:41-42

VIII.    **THE FALL AND GOD'S HOLINESS**

1.  **GOD'S HOLINESS**: "What comes into our minds when we think about God is the most important thing about us."[2] – A. W. Tozer

    1)  *"And He (Jesus) was saying to them, '**Take care what you listen to**. By your standard of measure it will be measured to you; and more will be given you besides."* – Mark 4:24 (emphasis added)

        •   In context to the Word being the seed of God.

    a)  Testimony of heaven:

        1)  *"And the four living creatures, each one of them having six wings, are full of eyes around and within; and **day and night they do not cease to say, "HOLY, HOLY, HOLY is THE LORD GOD, THE ALMIGHTY**, WHO WAS AND WHO IS AND WHO IS TO COME."* – Revelations 4:8

    b)  Testimony of God:

        1)  *"To whom then will you liken Me That I would be his equal?" says the Holy One."* – Isaiah 40:25

        2)  *"because it is written, "YOU SHALL BE HOLY, FOR I AM HOLY."* – 1 Peter 1:16

        3)  *"WHO COMMITTED NO SIN, NOR WAS ANY DECEIT FOUND IN HIS MOUTH."* – 1 Peter 2:22

---

[2] A. W. Tozer, *The Knowledge of the Holy* (New York: HarperCollins, 1961), 1.

c) Testimony of believers:

1) *"Who is like You among the gods, O LORD? Who is like You, **majestic in holiness**, Awesome in praises, working wonders?" – Exodus 15:11*

2) *"There is **no one** holy like the LORD, Indeed, there is no one besides You, Nor is there any rock like our God." – 1 Samuel 2:2*

3) *"For it was fitting for us to have such a high priest, **holy, innocent, undefiled**, separated from sinners and exalted above the heavens." – Hebrews 7:26*

d) Testimony of unbelievers:

1) *"So when the chief priests and the officers saw Him, they cried out saying, "Crucify, crucify!" Pilate said to them, "Take Him yourselves and crucify Him, for I find no guilt in Him." – John 19:6*

2) *"Which one of you convicts Me of sin?" – John 8:46*

e) Testimony of Jesus' life:

1) *"For it was fitting for us to have such a high priest, **holy, innocent, undefiled**, separated from sinners and exalted above the heavens." – Hebrews 7:26*

2) *"So when the chief priests and the officers saw Him, they cried out saying, "Crucify, crucify!" Pilate said to them, "Take Him yourselves and crucify Him, for I find no guilt in Him." John 19:6*

3) *"He made **Him who knew no sin** to be sin on our behalf, so that we might become the righteousness of God in Him." – 2 Corinthians 5:21*

2. **God's Righteous Judgment**: God is just. His attribute of justice does not conflict with any other attribute of His character, including His unconditional perfect love. God neither suspends one attribute of His character to carry out another. God is always just and loving.

   A) God's <u>ways</u> are perfect:

      1) *"<u>The sum of Your word is truth</u>, And <u>every one of Your righteous ordinances is everlasting</u>. Shin." – Psalms 119:160*

      2) *"And they sang the song of Moses, the bond-servant of God, and the song of the Lamb, saying, "Great and marvelous are Your works, O Lord God, the Almighty; <u>Righteous and true are Your ways</u>, King of the nations!" – Revelation 15:3*

   B) God's <u>judgments</u> are <u>perfect</u>, <u>accurate</u>, and <u>just</u>:

      1) *"What shall we say then? **There is no injustice with God**, is there? **May it never be**!" – Romans 9:14*

      2) *"BECAUSE <u>HIS JUDGMENTS ARE TRUE AND RIGHTEOUS</u>; for He has judged the great harlot who was corrupting the earth with her immorality, and HE HAS AVENGED THE BLOOD OF HIS BOND-SERVANTS ON HER." – Revelation 19:2*

      3) *"But <u>because of your stubbornness and unrepentant heart</u> you are storing up wrath for yourself in the*

day of wrath and _revelation of the_ **righteous judgment of God**." – Romans 2:5

4) "And I heard the altar saying, "Yes, O Lord God, the Almighty, _true and righteous are Your judgments._" – Revelation 16:7

C) We cannot bend God's righteous decision:

1) "Now then let the fear of the LORD be upon you; be very careful what you do, _for the LORD our God will have_ **no part in unrighteousness** _or_ **partiality** _or the_ **taking of a bribe**." – 2 Chronicles 19:7

2) "Opening his mouth, Peter said: "I **most certainly** _understand now that God is not one to show partiality._" – Acts 10:34

D) God judges unbelievers by their actions, including resistance of God's love, mercy, grace and hatred of His ways:

1) Actions:
   a) "Behold, I am coming quickly, and _My reward is with Me, to render to every man_ **according to what he has done**." – Revelation 22:12
2) Hatred and rejection of God's Word (ways):
   a) "But **because of your stubbornness and unrepentant heart** _you are storing up wrath for yourself in the day of wrath and revelation of the righteous judgment of God._" – Romans 2:5
   b) "**Why have you despised the word of the LORD** _by doing evil in His sight_? You have struck down Uriah the Hittite with the sword, have taken his wife to be

41

your wife, and have killed him with the sword of the sons of Ammon." – 2 Samuel 12:9

- Nathan is speaking to David.

c) *"For the sinful nature is always **hostile to God**. **It never** did **obey God's laws**, and **it never will**." – Romans 8:7, NLT*

3) Rejection of God's love, mercy, and grace:
   a) *"For **God so loved** the world, that He gave His only begotten Son, that **whoever believes in Him shall not perish**, but have eternal life." – John 3:16*
   b) *"Therefore **the LORD longs to be gracious to you**, And therefore He waits on high to have compassion on you. For the LORD is a God of justice; How blessed are all those who long for Him." – Isaiah 30:18*

   c) *"Jerusalem, Jerusalem, who kills the prophets and stones those who are sent to her! How often I wanted to gather your children together, the way a hen gathers her chicks under her wings, and **you were unwilling**." – Matthew 23:37*

   d) *"See to it that **no one comes short of the grace of God**; that no root of bitterness springing up causes trouble, and by it many be defiled." – Hebrews 12:15*

   e) *"**For they exchanged the truth of God for a lie**, and worshiped and served the creature rather than the Creator, who is blessed forever. Amen." – Romans 1:25*

E) **God's patience** before His judgments:
1) *"The LORD is slow to anger and abundant in lovingkindness, forgiving iniquity and transgression; but He will by no means clear the guilty, visiting the iniquity of the fathers on the children to the third and the fourth generations.'"* – Numbers 14:18

2) *"Then the LORD passed by in front of him and proclaimed, "The LORD, the LORD God, compassionate and gracious, slow to anger, and abounding in lovingkindness and truth."* – Exodus 34:6

3) *"Or do you think lightly of the riches of His kindness and tolerance and patience, not knowing that the kindness of God leads you to repentance?"* – Romans 2:4

4) *"Who once were disobedient, when the patience of God kept waiting in the days of Noah, during the construction of the ark, in which a few, that is, eight persons, were brought safely through the water."* – 1 Peter 3:20

5) *"The Lord is not slow about His promise, as some count slowness, but is patient toward you, not wishing for any to perish but for all to come to repentance."* – 2 Peter 3:9

6) *"Then in the fourth generation they will return here, for the iniquity of the Amorite is not yet complete."* – Genesis 15:16

7) *"Hindering us from speaking to the Gentiles so that they may be saved; with the result that they always*

*fill up the measure of their sins.* But wrath has come upon them to the utmost." – 1 Thessalonians 2:16

3. **The Fall of Man:**

   a) God made man upright:

      1) *"This only have I found: **God created mankind upright**, but they have gone in search of many schemes."* – Ecclesiastes 7:29, NIV

      2) *"God saw all that He had made, and behold, **it was very good**. And there was evening and there was morning, the sixth day."* – Genesis 1:31

   b) The Fall made all men made sinners through one act, the disobedience of Adam (Genesis chapter 3):

      1) *"For as through the one man's disobedience the many were made sinners, even so through the obedience of the One the many will be made righteous."* – Romans 5:19

   c) Because of the Fall, the **sin nature was inherited by all men**:

      1) *"For I know that nothing good dwells in me, **that is, in my flesh**; for the willing is present in me, but the doing of the good is not."* – Romans 7:18

      2) *"Thanks be to God through Jesus Christ our Lord! So then, on the one hand I myself with my mind am serving the law of God, but on the other, with my flesh the law of sin."* – Romans 7:25

3) *"For the flesh sets its desire against the Spirit, and the Spirit against the flesh; for these are in opposition to one another, so that you may not do the things that you please." – Galatians 5:17*

d) Physical and spiritual death (the Second Death, which is separation from God relational presence and eternal punishment):

1) *"But the free gift is not like the transgression. For if by the transgression of the one **the many died**, much more did the grace of God and the gift by the grace of the one Man, Jesus Christ, abound to the many." – Romans 5:15*

2) *"Therefore, just as through one man sin entered into the world, **and death through sin**, and **so death spread to all men, because all sinned.**" – Romans 5:12*

3) *"Nevertheless death reigned from Adam until Moses, even over those who had not sinned in the likeness of the offense of Adam, who is a type of Him who was to come." – Romans 5:14*

4) *"For as in Adam all die, so also in Christ all will be made alive." – 1 Corinthians 15:22*

5) *"He who has an ear, let him hear what the Spirit says to the churches. He who overcomes will not be hurt by the second death." – Revelation 2:11*

6) *"So then as through **one transgression** there **resulted condemnation to all men**, even so through one act of*

righteousness there resulted justification of life to all men." – Romans 5:18

e) All have rebelled against God and are in need of His mercy:

1) "Indeed, <u>there is not a righteous man on earth who continually does good and who never sins</u>." – Ecclesiastes 7:20

2) "But <u>the Scripture has **shut up everyone under sin**, so that the promise by faith in Jesus Christ might be given to those who believe."</u> – Galatians 3:22

3) "What then? <u>Are we better than they</u>? Not at all<u>; for we have already charged that both Jews and Greeks are **all under sin.**</u>" – Romans 3:9

4) "<u>For God has **shut up all in disobedience** so that He may show mercy to all.</u>" – Romans 11:32

5) "<u>Who can say, '**I have** cleansed my heart, I am pure from my sin?'</u>" – Proverbs 20:9

6) "For **all have sinned** and **fall short of the glory of God**." – Romans 3:23

7) "And Jesus said to him, "Why do you call Me good? **No one is good except God alone**." – Mark 10:18

## IX. JUSTIFICATION, OUR LEGAL POSITION:

### 1. REDEMPTION:

A) Christ took our punishment and paid the penalty for our sin:

1) *"And He Himself **is the propitiation for our sins**; and not for ours only, but also for those of the whole world." – 1 John 2:2*

2) *"Whom God displayed publicly **as a propitiation** in His blood through faith. This was to demonstrate His righteousness, because in the forbearance of God He passed over the sins previously committed." – Romans 3:25*

B) Christ **imputed righteousness** to those who believe:

1) *"So then as through one transgression there resulted condemnation to all men, even so through **one act of righteousness** there resulted justification of life to all men." – Romans 5:18*

2) *"Much more then, having now been justified by His blood, we shall be saved from the wrath of God through Him." – Romans 5:9*

3) *"But God demonstrates His own love toward us, in that **while we were yet sinners**, Christ died for us." – Romans 5:8*

4) *"For God **so loved the world**, that He gave His only begotten Son, that whoever believes in Him shall not perish, but have eternal life." – John 3:16*

C) We were enemies of God, and yet God loves His enemies:

1) *"For if **while we were enemies** we were reconciled to God through the death of His Son, much more, having been reconciled, we shall be saved by His life." –* Romans 5:10

2) *"But I say to you, love your enemies and pray for those who persecute you, so that you may be sons of your Father who is in heaven; for He causes His sun to rise on the evil and the good, and sends rain on the righteous and the unrighteous." – Matthew 5:44-45*

3) *"You adulteresses, do you not know that friendship with the world is **hostility toward God**? Therefore whoever wishes to be a friend of the world **makes himself an enemy of God.**" – James 4:4*

4) *"Do not love the world nor the things in the world. If anyone loves the world, the love of the Father is not in him." – 1 John 2:15*

5) *"**No one can serve two masters**; for either he will **hate** the one and **love** the other, or he will be **devoted** to one and **despise** the other. You cannot serve God and wealth." – Matthew 6:24*

6) *"Because the mind set on the flesh is **hostile toward God**; for it does not subject itself to the law of God, for it is not even able to do so." – Romans 8:7*

D) We could do nothing to help ourselves:

1) *"But God, being rich in mercy, because of **His great love with which He loved us**, even **when we were***

*dead in our transgressions, made us alive together with Christ (by grace you have been saved)." –* Ephesians 2:4-5

2) *"For while we were **still helpless**, at the right time Christ died for the ungodly." – Romans 5:6*

3) *"But God demonstrates His own love toward us, in that **while we were yet sinners**, Christ died for us." – Romans 5:8*

4) *"For by grace you have been saved through faith; and **that not of yourselves**, it is the gift of God." – Ephesians 2:8*

5) *"'Then who can be saved?' But He said, 'The things that are impossible with people are possible with God.'" – Luke 18:26-27*

6) *"So then it **does not depend on the man who wills or the man who runs**, but on God who has mercy." – Romans 9:16*

- "So then it is not of him that wills—hath the inward desire—nor of him that runs—makes active effort (compare 1 Cor. 9:24, 26; Philp. 2:16; 3:14). Both these are indispensable to salvation, yet salvation is owing to neither, but is purely "of God that shows mercy."[3] – Jamieson-Fausset-Brown Bible Commentary

---

[3] Robert Jamieson, A. R. Fausset, and David Brown, *Commentary, Critical, Practical, and Explanatory on the Old and New Testaments* (1882), accessed through:
http://biblehub.com/commentaries/romans/9-16.htm

Even our pursuit of God is the product of God's goodness, power, and grace and not our own ability.

E) Even our pursuit of God is the product of God's power, and grace:

1) *"**No one** can come to Me **unless the Father** who sent Me **draws him**; and I will raise him up on the last day." – John 6:44*

2) *"And He was saying, "For this reason I have said to you, that **no one** can come to Me **unless it has been granted him** from the Father." – John 6:65*

3) *"But God, being **rich in mercy**, because of **His great love with which He loved us**, even when we were dead in our transgressions, made us alive together with Christ (by grace you have been saved)." – Ephesians 2:4-5*

4) *"So then it **does not depend on the man who wills or the man who runs**, but on God who has mercy." – Romans 9:16*

F) God's sovereignty does not eliminate our free will but works within and with knowledge of our free will:

1) *Man's free will:*

   a) *"If **anyone is willing** to do His will, he will know of the teaching, whether it is of God or whether I speak from Myself." – John 7:17*

   b) *"You will seek Me and find Me **when you search for Me with all your heart**." – Jeremiah 29:13*

c) *"If it is disagreeable in your sight to serve the LORD, **choose for yourselves** today whom you will serve." – Joshua 24:15*

d) *"So Jesus said to the twelve, "**You do not want to go away also, do you**?" – John 6:67*

e) *"Submit therefore to God. Resist the devil and he will flee from you." – James 4:7*

2) *Man's rejection:*

   a) *"The LORD spoke to Manasseh and his people, but **they paid no attention**." – 2 Chronicles 33:10*

   b) *"And the LORD has sent to you all His servants the prophets **again and again**, but you have not listened nor inclined your ear to hear." – Jeremiah 25:4*

   c) *"And I set watchmen over you, saying, 'Listen to the sound of the trumpet!' **But they said, 'We will not listen**.'" – Jeremiah 6:17*

   d) *"Then he who hears the **sound of the trumpet and does not take warning**, and a sword comes and takes him away, his blood will be on his own head." – Ezekiel 33:4*

   e) *"O Jerusalem, Jerusalem, the city that kills the prophets and stones those sent to her! **How often I wanted** to gather your children together, just as a hen gathers her brood under her wings, and you would not have it!" – Luke 13:34*

f) *"from the blood of Abel to the blood of Zechariah, who was killed between the altar and the house of God; yes, I tell you, it shall be charged against this generation.'" – Luke 11:51*

g) *"I gave her time to repent, and she does not want to repent of her immorality." – Revelation 2:21*

3) *God's will for **all men to be saved**:*

   a) *"For God **so loved the world**, that He gave His only begotten Son, that whoever believes in Him shall not perish, but have eternal life." – John 3:16*

   b) *"This is good and acceptable in the sight of God our Savior, **who desires all men to be saved** and to come to the knowledge of the truth." – 1 Timothy 2:3-4*

   c) *"For the grace of God has appeared, bringing salvation to all men." – Titus 2:11*

   - Grace brought salvation within reach of all men, but more importantly it offered a reality to those who believe: *"Ho! Every one who thirsts, come to the waters; And you who have no money come, buy and eat. Come, buy wine and milk Without money and without cost" (Isaiah 55:1).*

   d) *"For it is for this we labor and strive, because we have fixed our hope on the living God, who is the Savior of all men, especially of believers." – 1 Timothy 4:10*

   - Jesus died for all men, even those who will reject His salvation and will not experience it.

e) *"Say to them, 'As I live!' declares the Lord GOD, **'I take no pleasure in the death of the wicked**, but rather that the wicked turn from his way and live. Turn back, turn back from your evil ways! Why then will you die, O house of Israel?'"* – Ezekiel 33:11

f) *"The Lord is not slow about His promise, as some count slowness, but is patient toward you, **not wishing for any to perish but for all to come to repentance**."* – 2 Peter 3:9

g) *"And they sang a new song, saying, "Worthy are You to take the book and to break its seals; **for You were slain, and purchased for God with Your blood men from every tribe and tongue and people and nation.**"* – Revelation 5:9

4) God is at liberty to use those who reject His salvation to save those who will receive His salvation:

a) *"Then the LORD said to Moses, 'Rise up early in the morning and stand before Pharaoh and say to him, **'Thus says the LORD**, the God of the Hebrews, 'Let My people go, that they may serve Me. 'For this time I will send all My plagues on you and your servants and your people, **so that you may know that there is no one like Me in all the earth.** 'For if by now I had put forth My hand and struck you and your people with pestilence, you would then have been cut off from the earth. 'But, indeed, **for this reason I have allowed you to remain**, in order **to show you My power** and in order **to proclaim My name through all the earth.** 'Still you exalt yourself*

against *My people by not letting them go.'"* —
*Exodus 9:13-17*

b) *"For the Scripture says to Pharaoh, 'FOR THIS VERY*
*PURPOSE I RAISED YOU UP, TO DEMONSTRATE MY*
*POWER IN YOU, AND **THAT MY NAME MIGHT BE***
***PROCLAIMED THROUGHOUT THE WHOLE EARTH.**'"*
— *Romans 9:17*

c) *"What if God, although willing to demonstrate His*
*wrath and to make His power known, **endured with***
***much patience vessels of wrath prepared for***
***destruction**?" — Romans 9:22*

d) *"Or does not the potter have a right over the clay, to*
*make from the same lump one vessel for honorable*
*use and another for common use?" — Romans 9:21*

e) *After these things I looked, and behold, **a great***
***multitude which no one could count**, from **every***
***nation** and **all tribes** and **peoples and tongues**,*
*standing before the throne and before the Lamb,*
*clothed in white robes, and palm branches were in*
*their hands; and they cry out with a loud voice,*
*saying, '**Salvation to our God** who sits on the*
*throne, and to the Lamb.'... 'These are the ones **who***
***come out of the great tribulation**, and they have*
*washed their robes and made them white in the*
*blood of the Lamb.'" — Revelation 7:9-10,14*

f) *"At night my soul longs for You, Indeed, my spirit*
*within me seeks You diligently; **For when the earth***
***experiences Your judgments The inhabitants of the***
***world learn righteousness**." — Isaiah 26:9*

54

g) *"And just as they did not see fit to acknowledge God any longer, **God gave them over to a depraved mind**, to do those things which are not proper." – Romans 1:28*

5) God's perfect, unconditional love does not mean everyone will be saved:

   a) *"Enter through the narrow gate; for **the gate is wide and the way is broad that leads to destruction**, and there are many who enter through it. For **the gate is small** and **the way is narrow that leads to life**, and there are **few who find i**t." – Matthew 7:13-14*

   b) *"**How will we escape if we neglect so great a salvation**? After it was at the first spoken through the Lord, it was confirmed to us by those who heard." – Hebrews 2:3*

   c) *"THIS PEOPLE HONORS ME WITH THEIR LIPS, BUT THEIR HEART IS FAR AWAY FROM ME." – Matthew 15:8*

   d) *"**Many will say to Me on that day**, 'Lord, Lord, did we not prophesy in Your name, and in Your name cast out demons, and in Your name perform many miracles?' And then I will declare to them, '**I never knew you; DEPART FROM ME, YOU WHO PRACTICE LAWLESSNESS**.'" – Matthew 7:22-23*

   e) *"Who once were disobedient, **when the patience of God kept waiting in the days of Noah**, during the construction of the ark, in which a few, that is, eight persons, were brought safely through the water." – 1 Peter 3:20*

## X. WHAT IS SIN:

1. <u>Whatever is done in love</u> (as define by God's holy and pure love) **is not sin**. Love is not an excuse to dismiss the law, but love is the essence of the law, and love in action is the carrying out of the law:

   a) *"'Teacher, which is the great commandment in the Law?' And He said to him, '**YOU SHALL LOVE THE LORD** YOUR GOD WITH ALL YOUR HEART, AND WITH ALL YOUR SOUL, AND WITH ALL YOUR MIND.' 'This is the great and foremost commandment. The second is like it, '**YOU SHALL LOVE YOUR NEIGHBOR AS YOURSELF.'** <u>On these two commandments</u> **depend the whole Law and the Prophets."** – Matthew 22:36-40*

   b) *"**To the pure, all things are pure**; <u>but to those who are defiled and unbelieving, nothing is pure</u>, but both their mind and their conscience are defiled."* – Titus 1:15

   c) *"But the **fruit of the Spirit** is **love, joy, peace, patience, kindness, goodness, faithfulness, gentleness, self-control; against such things there is no law**."* – Galatians 5:22-23

   d) *"**Love is patient, love is kind** and **is not jealous; love does not brag** and **is not arrogant, does not act unbecomingly; it does not seek its own, is not provoked, does not take into account a wrong suffered, does not rejoice in unrighteousness, but rejoices with the truth; bears all things, believes all***

things, _hopes all things, endures all things._" – 1
Corinthians 13:4-7

2.  Anything not done in faith is sin:

a)  "**Whatever is not from faith is sin**." – Romans 14:23

b)  "**Concerning sin, because they do not believe in
    Me**." – John 16:9

c)  "He who believes in Him is not judged; **he who does
    not believe has been judged already, because he
    has not believed in the name of the only begotten
    Son of God**." – John 3:18

3.  **ORIGIN OF SIN: Sin comes from the heart:**

a)  "**For out of the heart come evil thoughts**, _murders,
    adulteries, fornications, thefts, false witness,
    slanders._ '**These are the things which defile the
    man**;'" – Matthew 15:19-20

b)  "**Watch over your heart with all diligence**, For from
    it flow the springs of life." – Proverbs 4:23

c)  "but I say to you that everyone who looks at a
    woman with lust for her _has already committed
    adultery with her_ **in his heart**." – Matthew 5:28

d)  "The good man out of the good treasure of his heart
    brings forth what is good; and the evil man out of
    the evil treasure brings forth what is evil; **for his
    mouth speaks from that which fills his heart**." –
    Luke 6:45

e) *"THIS PEOPLE HONORS ME WITH THEIR LIPS, **BUT THEIR HEART IS FAR AWAY FROM ME**." – Matthew 15:8*

f) *"But if you had known what this means, '**I DESIRE COMPASSION (covenant love), AND NOT A SACRIFICE,**' you would not have condemned the innocent." – Matthew 12:7, (emphasis added)*

g) *"**The heart is more deceitful than all else and is desperately sick**; Who can understand it?" – Jeremiah 17:9*

4. When we have saving faith, there is a transformation in our heart which leads to a new relationship with sin:

a) *"Therefore **if anyone is in Christ, he is a new creature**; the old things passed away; behold, **new things have come**." – 2 Corinthians 5:17*

b) *"Moreover, **I will give you a new heart and put a new spirit within you**; and **I will remove the heart of stone** from your flesh and give you a heart of flesh." – Ezekiel 36:26*

c) *"Jesus answered and said to him, "Truly, truly, I say to you, **unless one is born again he cannot see the kingdom of God**." – John 3:3*

d) *"Being manifested that you are a letter of Christ, cared for by us, written not with ink **but with the Spirit of the living God, not on tablets of stone but on tablets of human hearts**." – 2 Corinthians 3:3*

e) *"**Create in me a clean heart**, O God, And renew a steadfast spirit within me." – Psalms 51:10*

f) *"But I tell you the truth, it is to your advantage that I go away; for if I do not go away, **the Helper** will not come to you; but if I go, I will send Him to you. 'And He, when He comes, **will convict the world concerning sin** and **righteousness** and **judgment**.'" – John 16:7-8*

5. Believers are to obey moral law:

a) *"**But (sexual) immorality** or **any** impurity or greed must not even be named among you, as is proper among **saints**." – Ephesians 5:3 (emphasis added)*

b) *"Or do you not know that the **unrighteous will not inherit the kingdom of God**? Do not be deceived; neither **fornicators**, nor **idolaters**, nor **adulterers**, nor **effeminate**, nor **homosexuals**, nor **thieves**, nor the **covetous**, nor **drunkards**, nor **revilers**, nor **swindlers**, **will inherit the kingdom of God**. **Such were some of you**; but you were washed, but you were sanctified, but you were justified in the name of the Lord Jesus Christ and in the Spirit of our God." – 1 Corinthians 6:9-11*

c) *"Now the deeds of the flesh are evident, which are: **immorality**, **impurity**, **sensuality**, **idolatry**, **sorcery**, **enmities**, **strife**, **jealousy**, **outbursts of anger**, **disputes**, **dissensions**, **factions**, **envying**, **drunkenness**, **carousing**, and things like these, of which I forewarn you, just as I have forewarned you,* *that those who practice such things will not inherit the kingdom of God." – Galatians 5:19-21*

6.  We have been set free from sin:

a)  *"**For sin shall not be master over you**, for you are not under law but under grace." – Romans 6:14*

b)  *"Therefore **do not let sin reign in your mortal body so that you obey its lusts**" – Romans 6:12*

c)  *"Now the Lord is the Spirit, and **where the Spirit of the Lord is, there is liberty.**" – 2 Corinthians 3:17*

d)  *"**So if the Son makes you free, you will be free indeed**." – John 8:36*

e)  *"**It was for freedom that Christ set us free**; therefore keep standing firm and **do not be subject again to a yoke of slavery.**" – Galatians 5:1*

f)  *"THE SPIRIT OF THE LORD IS UPON ME, BECAUSE HE ANOINTED ME TO PREACH THE GOSPEL TO THE POOR. **HE HAS SENT ME TO PROCLAIM RELEASE TO THE CAPTIVES**, AND RECOVERY OF SIGHT TO THE BLIND, **TO SET FREE THOSE WHO ARE OPPRESSED**," – Luke 4:18*

g)  *"**For He rescued us from the domain of darkness**, and transferred us to the kingdom of His beloved Son." – Colossians 1:13*

h)  *"For the LORD your God is living among you. **He is a mighty savior**. He will take delight in you with gladness. With his love, he will calm all your fears.*

*He will rejoice over you with joyful songs." —*
*Zephaniah 3:17, NLT*

i) *"Therefore **He is able to save completely** those who come to God through him, because he always lives to intercede for them." — Hebrews 7:25, NIV*

7. We should not open a door to sin after Christ has delivered us:

a) *"If you do well, will not your countenance be lifted up? And if you do not do well, **sin is crouching at the door; and its desire is for you, but you must master it.**" — Genesis 4:7*

b) *"But each one is tempted **when he is carried away and enticed by his own lust**. Then when lust has conceived, it gives birth to sin; and when sin is accomplished, it brings forth death." — James 1:14-15*

c) *"For if, after they have escaped the defilements of the world by the knowledge of the Lord and Savior Jesus Christ, they are again entangled in them and are overcome, **the last state has become worse for them than the first**. For it would be better for them not to have known the way of righteousness, than having known it, to turn away from the holy commandment handed on to them." — 2 Peter 2:20-21*

- It is detrimental to our spiritual health when God reveals Himself and we feel no conviction resisting Him.

d) *"Now <u>when the unclean spirit goes out of a man</u>, it passes through waterless places seeking rest, and does not find it. "Then it says, 'I will return to my house from which I came'; and when it comes, <u>it finds it unoccupied</u>, swept, and put in order. "**<u>Then it goes and takes along with it seven other spirits more wicked than itself, and they go in and live there; and the last state of that man becomes worse than the first.</u>** That is the way it will also be with this evil generation." – Matthew 12:43-45*

e) *"**<u>It was for freedom that Christ set us free</u>**; therefore keep standing firm and **<u>do not be subject again to a yoke of slavery</u>**." – Galatians 5:1*

8. How we should see our self:

   a) "Even **so consider yourselves** to be **dead to sin, but alive to God in Christ Jesus**." – Romans 6:11

   b) *"<u>Therefore **consider the members of your earthly body as dead to**</u> immorality, impurity, passion, evil desire, and greed, which amounts to idolatry. For it is because of these things that the wrath of God will come upon the sons of disobedience." – Colossians 3:5-6*

9. The Lord is able to keep us from stumbling:

   a) *"**<u>Now to Him who is able to keep you from stumbling</u>**, and to make you stand in the presence of His glory blameless with great joy." – Jude 1:24*

   b) *"Therefore, brethren, <u>be all the more diligent to make certain about His calling and choosing you;</u> **for*** *as long as you practice these things, you will never stumble."* — 2 Peter 1:10

c) *"**Now to Him who is able to establish you** according to my gospel and the preaching of Jesus Christ, according to the revelation of the mystery which has been kept secret for long ages past."* — Romans 16:25

d) *"seeing that His divine power **has granted** to us **everything pertaining to life and godliness**, through the true knowledge of Him who called us by His own glory and excellence"* — 2 Peter 1:3

**10. We can be strong in the Lord:**

a) *"Finally, **be strong in the Lord and in the strength of His might.**"* — Ephesians 6:10

b) *"**Now to Him who is able to establish you** according to my gospel and the preaching of Jesus Christ, according to the revelation of the mystery which has been kept secret for long ages past."* — Romans 16:25

c) *"Be on the alert, **stand firm in the faith, act like men, be strong**."* — 1 Corinthians 16:13

d) *"That He would grant you, according to the riches of His glory, **to be strengthened with power through His Spirit in the inner man**."* — Ephesians 3:16

e) *"And He has said to me, "**My grace is sufficient for you, for power is perfected in weakness.**" Most gladly, therefore, **I will rather boast about my***

**weaknesses, so that the power of Christ may dwell in me.**" – 2 Corinthians 12:9

f) "**I can do all things through Him who strengthens me**." – Philippians 4:13

g) "Therefore **everyone who hears these words of Mine and acts on them**, may be compared to a **wise man who built his house on the rock**. And the rain fell, and the floods came, and the winds blew and slammed against that house; and **yet it did not fall, for it had been founded on the rock**." – Matthew 7:24-25

11. Believers still experience temptation, but now they have the ability to resist temptation:

a) "No temptation has overtaken you but such as is common to man; and **God is faithful**, who **will not allow you to be tempted beyond what you are able**, but with the temptation **will provide the way of escape** also, so that **you will be able to endure it**." – 1 Corinthians 10:13

b) "**Pray, then, in this way**...**And do not lead us into temptation, but deliver us from evil**. For Yours is the kingdom and the power and the glory forever. Amen." – Matthew 6:9,13

c) "I do not ask You to take them out of the world, **but to keep them from the evil one**." – John 17:15

d) "**But the Lord is faithful**, and **He will strengthen and protect you from the evil one**." – 2 Thessalonians 3:3

12. Being free from sin means being a slave to God:

a) *"Or **do you not know that your body is a temple of the Holy Spirit who is in you**, whom you have from God, and that **you are not your own**? For <u>you have been bought with a price</u>: **therefore glorify God in your body.**" – 1 Corinthians 6:19-20*

b) *"Do you not know that when you present yourselves to someone as slaves for obedience, **you are slaves of the one whom you obey, either of sin resulting in death, or of obedience resulting in righteousness?**" – Romans 6:16*

c) *"Therefore I urge you, brethren, by the mercies of God, **to present your bodies a living and holy sacrifice, acceptable to God, which is your spiritual service of worship.**" – Romans 12:1*

13. **Those that are led by the Holy Spirit** are **not bound by the law**. The Holy Spirit will not lead us to break the moral law:

a) *"But if you are led by the Spirit, you are not under the Law." – Galatians 5:18*

- The Holy Spirit will not lead us into moral turpitude.

14. **Believers do not practice unrepentant habitual sin:**

a) *"What shall we say then? <u>Are we to continue in sin so that grace may increase</u>? **May it never be**! How shall we **who died to sin still live in it**?" – Romans 6:1-2*

65

b) *"What then? **Shall we sin because we are not under law but under grace? May it never be**!" – Romans 6:15*

c) *"Act as free men, and **do not use your freedom as a covering for evil**, but use it as bondslaves of God." – 1 Peter 2:16*

d) *"**But now having been freed from sin and enslaved to God**, you derive your benefit, resulting in sanctification, and the outcome, eternal life." – Romans 6:22*

e) *"**For you were called to freedom**, brethren; **only do not turn your freedom into an opportunity for the flesh**, but through love serve one another." – Galatians 5:13*

f) *"Jesus answered them, "Truly, truly, I say to you, **everyone who commits sin is the slave of sin.**" – John 8:34*

   - Everyone who lives in unrepentant sin is a slave to sin.

g) *"For if we **go on sinning willfully** after receiving the knowledge of the truth, **there no longer remains a sacrifice for sins**," Hebrews 10:26*

h) *"And do not go on presenting the members of your body to sin as instruments of unrighteousness; **but present yourselves to God as those alive from the dead, and your members as instruments of righteousness to God**." – Romans 6:13*

i) *"**We know that no one who is born of God sins**; but He who was born of God keeps him, and the evil one does not touch him." – 1 John 5:18*

- Sins, plural: practices unrepentant habitual sin.

15. We are aware of what sin is:

a) *"And **although they know the ordinance of God**, that those who practice such things are worthy of death, **they not only do the same**, but also give hearty approval to those who practice them." – Romans 1:32*

b) *"For the wrath of God is revealed from heaven against all ungodliness and unrighteousness of **men who suppress the truth in unrighteousness.**" – Romans 1:18*

c) *"**For they exchanged the truth of God for a lie**, and worshiped and served the creature rather than the Creator, who is blessed forever. Amen." – Romans 1:25*

d) *"Because that which is known about God **is evident within them**; **for God made it evident to them.** For since the creation of the world His invisible attributes, His eternal power and divine nature, **have been clearly seen**, being understood through what has been made, **so that they are without excuse. For even though they knew God**, they did not honor Him as God or give thanks, but they became futile in their speculations, and their foolish heart was darkened. Professing to be wise, they became fools." – Romans 1:19-21*

e) *"For when Gentiles who do not have the Law do instinctively the things of the Law, these, not having the Law, **are a law to themselves, in that they show the work of the Law written in their hearts**, their conscience bearing witness and their thoughts alternately accusing or else defending them."* – Romans 2:14-15

f) *"**Therefore you have no excuse**, everyone of you who passes judgment, for in that which you judge another, you condemn yourself; **for you who judge practice the same things**."* – Romans 2:1

g) *"But I tell you the truth, it is to your advantage that I go away; for if I do not go away, **the Helper** will not come to you; but if I go, I will send Him to you. 'And He, when He comes, **will convict the world concerning sin** and **righteousness** and **judgment**.'"* – John 16:7-8

16. Sin leads to death, hell, punishment, and eternal separation from God's relational presence:

a) *"**For the wages of sin is death**, but the free gift of God is eternal life in Christ Jesus our Lord."* – Romans 6:23

17. Sin separates us from a relational presence with God:

a) *"They heard the sound of the LORD God walking in the garden in the cool of the day, and the man and his wife **hid themselves from the presence of the LORD God** among the trees of the garden. Then the LORD*

*God called to the man, and said to him, 'Where are you?'" – Genesis 3:8-9*

b) *"But your iniquities have made a separation between you and your God, And your sins have hidden His face from you so that He does not hear." – Isaiah 59:2*

c) *"Surely your goodness and unfailing love will pursue me all the days of my life, and I will live in the house of the LORD forever." – Psalms 23:6, NLT*

- Even within a broken relationship, God pursues us.

d) *"But in all these things we overwhelmingly conquer through Him who loved us. For I am convinced that neither death, nor life, nor angels, nor principalities, nor things present, nor things to come, nor powers, nor height, nor depth, nor any other created thing, will be able to separate us from the love of God, which is in Christ Jesus our Lord." – Romans 8:37-39*

- Love does not imply a saving relationship with God.

18. There should be notable distinction between believers and unbelievers:

a) *"But actually, I wrote to you not to associate with any so-called brother if he is an immoral person, or covetous, or an idolater, or a reviler, or a drunkard, or a swindler-- not even to eat with such a one." – 1 Corinthians 5:11*

b) *"For there must also be factions among you, <u>so that those who are approved may become evident among you</u>." – 1 Corinthians 11:19*

c) *"When you pray, **you are not to be like the hypocrites**; for they love to stand and pray in the synagogues and on the street corners so that they may be seen by men. Truly I say to you, they have their reward in full." – Matthew 6:5*

d) *"**Do not worry then, saying**, 'What will we eat?' or 'What will we drink?' or 'What will we wear for clothing?' **For the Gentiles eagerly seek all these things**; for your heavenly Father knows that you need all these things. But seek first His kingdom and His righteousness, and all these things will be added to you." – Matthew 6:31-33*

e) *"For if you love those who love you, what reward do you have? **Do not even the tax collectors do the same?** If you greet only your brothers, **what more are you doing than others? Do not even the Gentiles do the same? Therefore you are to be perfect, as your heavenly Father is perfect**." – Matthew 5:46-48*

19. <u>**OUR STANCE** TOWARDS **UNGODLY FLESHLY DESIRES, SIN**, AND **SATAN** IS ONE OF **WAR:**</u>

   a) We are AT WAR WITH UNGODLY FLESHLY DESIRES, SIN, AND SATAN:

   1) *"Finally, **be strong in the Lord** and **in the strength of His might. Put on** the **full armor of God**, so that you will be able to **stand firm against the schemes***

*__of the devil__. For our struggle __is not against flesh and blood__, but __against the rulers, against the powers, against the world forces of this darkness, against the spiritual forces of wickedness in the heavenly places__. Therefore, take up the full armor of God, so __that you will be able to resist in the evil day__, and __having done everything, to stand firm__. __Stand firm__ therefore, HAVING GIRDED YOUR LOINS WITH TRUTH, and HAVING PUT ON THE BREASTPLATE OF RIGHTEOUSNESS, and having shod YOUR FEET WITH THE PREPARATION OF THE GOSPEL OF PEACE; in addition to all, taking up the shield of faith with which you will be able to extinguish all the flaming arrows of the evil one. And take THE HELMET OF SALVATION, and the sword of the Spirit, which is the word of God. With all prayer and petition pray at all times in the Spirit, and with this in view, __be on the alert__ with all perseverance and petition for all the saints." – Ephesians 6:10-18*

2) *"For the flesh __sets its desire against__ the Spirit, and the Spirit __against the flesh__; for __these are in opposition to one another__, so that you may not do the things that you please." – Galatians 5:17*

3) *"Because the __mind set on the flesh is hostile toward God__; for it __does not subject itself to the law of God__, for __it is not even able to do so__." – Romans 8:7*

71

4) *"Be of sober spirit, **be on the alert**. **Your adversary, the devil,** prowls around like a roaring lion, **seeking someone to devour**."* – 1 Peter 5:8

5) *"So that no advantage would be taken of us by Satan, for we are **not ignorant of his schemes**."* – 2 Corinthians 2:11

6) *"Simon, Simon, behold, **Satan has demanded permission to sift you like wheat.**"* – Luke 22:31

7) *"**Submit therefore to God. Resist the devil** and he will flee from you."* James 4:7

8) *"And **do not give the devil an opportunity**."* – Ephesians 4:27

9) *"These are the ones who are beside the road where the word is sown; and when they hear, immediately **Satan comes and takes away the word** which has been sown in them."* – Mark 4:15

10) *"**The thief comes only to steal and kill and destroy**; I came that they may have life, and have it abundantly."* – John 10:10

11) *"Or how can anyone enter the strong man's house and carry off his property, **unless he first binds the strong man? And then he will plunder his house.**"* – Matthew 12:29

12) *"If you do well, will not your countenance be lifted up? And if you do not do well, **sin is crouching at the door; and its desire is for you, but you must master it**."* – Genesis 4:7

b) We are to flee from sin:

1) *"And do not get drunk with wine, for that is dissipation, but be filled with the Spirit." – Ephesians 5:18*

2) *"**Flee (sexual) immorality**. Every other sin that a man commits is outside the body, but the immoral man sins against his own body." – 1 Corinthians 6:18 (emphasis added)*

3) *"Therefore, my beloved, **flee from idolatry**." – 1 Corinthians 10:14*

20. False teaching:

a) *"**But false prophets also arose** among the people, just as **there will also be false teachers among you**, who **will secretly introduce destructive heresies**, even denying the Master who bought them, bringing swift destruction upon themselves." – 2 Peter 2:1*

b) *"But the **Spirit explicitly says** that in later times **some will fall away from the faith, paying attention to deceitful spirits** and **doctrines of demons**." – 1 Timothy 4:1*

c) *"That they were saying to you, "In the last time **there will be mockers**, following after their own ungodly lusts." – Jude 1:18*

d) *"For the time will come when **they will not endure sound doctrine**; but wanting to have their ears tickled, **they will accumulate for themselves***

***teachers*** *in accordance to their own desires." – 2 Timothy 4:3*

e) *"Beloved, while I was making every effort to write you about our common salvation, I felt the necessity to write to you appealing that **you contend earnestly for the faith** which was once for all handed down to the saints. For certain persons **have crept in unnotic**ed, those who were long beforehand marked out for this condemnation, **ungodly persons** who **turn the grace of our God into licentiousness** and deny our only Master and Lord, Jesus Christ." – Jude 1:3-4*

f) *"Many will **follow their sensuality**, and **because of them the way of the truth will be maligned**." – 2 Peter 2:2*

g) *"For 'THE NAME OF GOD IS BLASPHEMED AMONG THE GENTILES BECAUSE OF YOU,' just as it is written." – Romans 2:24*

h) *"To the pure, all things are pure; but to those who are **defiled** and **unbelieving**, **nothing is pure**, but **both their mind and their conscience are defiled. They profess to know God, but by their deeds they deny Him, being detestable** and **disobedient** and worthless for any good deed." – Titus 1:15-16*

21. Not everyone will be forgiven. There has to be repentance:

a) *"Therefore I said to you that you will die in your sins;* ***for unless you believe that I am He, you will die in your sins.***" – *John 8:24*

b) *"We know that* <u>*God does not hear sinners;*</u> ***but if anyone is God-fearing and does His will, He hears him***." – *John 9:31*

c) *"He who* <u>*turns away his ear from listening to the law,*</u> ***Even his prayer is an abomination.***" – *Proverbs 28:9*

d) *"**If I regard wickedness in my heart,*** <u>The Lord will not hear;</u>" *Psalms 66:18*

e) *"**The sacrifice of the wicked is an abomination,*** <u>How much more when he brings it with evil intent!</u>" – *Proverbs 21:27*

f) *"And said, "Truly I say to you,* ***unless you are converted and become like children,*** <u>you will not enter the kingdom of heaven.</u>" – *Matthew 18:3*

g) *"And Jesus said to them, '* <u>Do you suppose that these Galileans were greater sinners than all other Galileans because they suffered this fate?</u> ***I tell you, no, but unless you repent, you will all likewise perish.***'" – *Luke 13:2-3*

h) *"*<u>Bring your worthless offerings no longer, Incense is an abomination to Me. New moon and sabbath, the</u>

*calling of assemblies-- I cannot endure iniquity and the solemn assembly." – Isaiah 1:13*

i) *"'Oh that there were one among you who would shut the gates, that you might not uselessly kindle fire on My altar! I am not pleased with you,' says the LORD of hosts, 'nor will I accept an offering from you.'" – Malachi 1:10*

j) *"If we confess our sins, He is faithful and righteous to forgive us our sins and to cleanse us from all unrighteousness." – 1 John 1:9*

k) *"Go and proclaim these words toward the north and say, 'Return, faithless Israel,' declares the LORD; 'I will not look upon you in anger. **For I am gracious,' declares the LORD; 'I will not be angry forever. 'Only acknowledge your iniquity**, that you have transgressed against the LORD your God and have scattered your favors to the strangers under every green tree, and you have not obeyed My voice,' declares the LORD." – Jeremiah 3:12-13*

l) *"**How blessed is he whose transgression is forgiven, whose sin is covered**! How blessed is the man to whom the LORD does not impute iniquity, and in whose spirit there is no deceit! **When I kept silent about my sin, my body wasted away through my groaning all day long**. For day and night Your hand was heavy upon me; my vitality was drained away as with the fever heat of summer. **Selah. I acknowledged my sin to You, and my iniquity I did not hide; I said, "I will confess my transgressions to***

*the LORD"; and You forgave the guilt of my sin." –*
*Psalms 32:1-5*

22.  Jesus and the apostles talked about hell with boldness
     and compassion:

   a)  *"And you, Capernaum, will not be exalted to heaven,
       will you? You will descend to Hades; for if the
       miracles had occurred in Sodom which occurred in
       you, it would have remained to this day." –
       Matthew 11:23*

   b)  *"In Hades he lifted up his eyes, being in torment,
       and saw Abraham far away and Lazarus in his
       bosom. 'And he cried out and said, 'Father
       Abraham, have mercy on me, and send Lazarus so
       that he may dip the tip of his finger in water and
       cool off my tongue, for I am in agony in this flame.'
       'But Abraham said, 'Child, remember that during
       your life you received your good things, and likewise
       Lazarus bad things; but now he is being comforted
       here, and you are in agony. 'And besides all this,
       between us and you there is a great chasm fixed, so
       that those who wish to come over from here to you
       will not be able, and that none may cross over from
       there to us.' 'And he said, 'Then I beg you, father,
       that you send him to my father's house—for I have
       five brothers—in order that he may warn them, so
       that they will not also come to this place of
       torment.'" – Luke 16:23-28*

   c)  *"You serpents, you brood of vipers, how will you
       escape the sentence of hell?" – Matthew 23:33*

d) *"In that place there will be weeping and gnashing of teeth when you see Abraham and Isaac and Jacob and all the prophets in the kingdom of God, but yourselves being thrown out."* – Luke 13:28

e) *"Then the king said to the servants, 'Bind him hand and foot, and throw him into the outer darkness; in that place there will be weeping and gnashing of teeth.'"* – Matthew 22:13

f) *"But as he was discussing <u>righteousness, self-control</u> **and the judgment to come**, Felix became frightened and said, 'Go away for the present, and when I find time I will summon you.'"* – Acts 24:25

g) *"And He, when He comes, <u>will convict the world concerning sin</u> and <u>righteousness</u> **and judgment**."* – John 16:8

23. Degrees of sin:

a) All sin is the same in that we are in need of a savior:

1) *"<u>For whoever</u> **keeps the whole law** <u>and yet</u> **stumbles in one point**, he has become **guilty of all**."* – James 2:10

b) There are degrees of bondage of sin and rebellion:

1) *"Jesus answered, 'You would have no authority over Me, unless it had been given you from above; for this reason <u>he who delivered Me to you has</u> **the greater sin**.'"* – John 19:11

2) *"Yet <u>you have not merely walked in their ways or done according to their abominations</u>; but, as if that*

78

were too little, **you acted more corruptly in all your conduct than they**." – Ezekiel 16:47

3) *"There are six things which the LORD hates, yes, **seven which are an abomination to Him**: haughty eyes, a lying tongue, and hands that shed innocent blood, a heart that devises wicked plans, feet that run rapidly to evil, a false witness who utters lies, and one who spreads strife among brothers."* – Proverbs 6:16-19

4) *"You shall not lie with a male as one lies with a female; it is an abomination."* – Leviticus 18:22

24. Greater judgment is reserved for greater sin:

1) *"Woe to you, scribes and Pharisees, hypocrites, because you devour widows' houses, and for a pretense you make long prayers; **therefore you will receive greater condemnation**."* – Matthew 23:14

2) *"Then in the fourth generation they will return here, **for the iniquity of the Amorite is not yet complete** (full)."* Genesis 15:16 (emphasis added)

3) *"In their effort to keep us from speaking to the Gentiles so that they may be saved. **In this way they always heap up their sins to the limit**. The wrath of God has come upon them at last."* – 1 Thessalonians 2:16, NIV

25. Greater revelation and stewardship leads to greater responsibility and judgment:

   1) *"Whoever does not receive you, nor heed your words, as you go out of that house or that city, shake the dust off your feet. Truly I say to you, **it will be more tolerable for the land of Sodom and Gomorrah in the day of judgment than for that city**." – Matthew 10:14-15*

   2) *"But the one who did not know it, and committed deeds worthy of a flogging, will receive but few. **From everyone who has been given much, much will be required; and to whom they entrusted much, of him they will ask all the more**." – Luke 12:48*

26. Deliberate sin leads to great transgression:

   1) *"Keep your servant also from willful sins; may they not rule over me. **Then I will be blameless, innocent of great transgression**." – Psalms 19:13,* NIV

27. Sin starts with the eyes, ears, and thought life:

   1) *"But each one is tempted when he is **carried away** and **enticed by his own lust**." – James 1:14*

   2) *"When the woman **saw** that the tree was good for food, and that **it was a delight to the eyes**, and that the tree was desirable to make one wise, she took from its fruit and ate; and she gave also to her husband with her, and he ate." – Genesis 3:6*

3) *"For all that is in the world, the lust of the flesh and the lust of the eyes and the boastful pride of life, is not from the Father, but is from the world."* – *1 John 2:16*

4) *"Again, <u>the devil took Him to a very high mountain and showed Him all the kingdoms of the world and their glory;</u>" Matthew 4:8*

5) *"But I say to you that everyone who <u>looks at a woman with lust for her has already committed adultery with her in his heart</u>."* – *Matthew 5:28*

28. Sinful thoughts, when meditated on, enter our heart and become a stronghold:

1) *"We are destroying speculations and <u>every lofty thing raised up against the knowledge of God</u>, and <u>we are taking every thought captive to the obedience of Christ,</u>" 2 Corinthians 10:5*

2) *"But I say to you that <u>everyone who looks at a woman with lust for her has already committed adultery with her in his heart</u>."* – *Matthew 5:28*

3) *"For <u>out of the heart come evil thoughts</u>, murders, adulteries, fornications, thefts, false witness, slanders."* – *Matthew 15:19*

29. Unaddressed sinful thoughts turn into greater bondage of physical acts:

1) *"Then the <u>LORD saw that the wickedness of man was great on the earth, and that every intent of</u>*

*the thoughts of his heart was only evil continually." – Genesis 6:5*

2) *"Or how can anyone enter the strong man's house and carry off his property, unless he first binds the strong man? And then he will plunder his house." –* Matthew 12:29

3) *"You brood of vipers, how can you, being evil, speak what is good? For the mouth speaks out of that which fills the heart." – Matthew 12:34*

**30. Guarding our hearts from sin:**

1) Taking extreme measures with sin:

   A. *"If your right eye makes you stumble, tear it out and throw it from you; for it is better for you to lose one of the parts of your body, than for your whole body to be thrown into hell." – Matthew 5:29*

   • Not talking about self-mutilation, but going to the extreme with sin.

2) Counterattack anxiety with prayer:

   A. *"Be anxious for nothing, but in everything by prayer and supplication with thanksgiving let your requests be made known to God. And the peace of God, which surpasses all comprehension, will guard your hearts and your minds in Christ Jesus." – Philippians 4:6-7*

3) Be proactive and intentional about guarding your heart:

a) *"**Watch over your heart with all diligence**, For from it flow the springs of life." – Proverbs 4:23*

4) Make a clearly defined covenant with eyes:

a) *"**I have made a covenant with my eyes**; How then could I gaze at a virgin?" – Job 31:1*

5) Identifying the small compromises in our lives that hinder love:

a) *"Catch the foxes for us, **The little foxes that are ruining the vineyards**, While our vineyards are in blossom." – Songs 2:15*

## XI. SAVING FAITH, SAVING GRACE, SAVING KNOWLEDGE, OUR LOVE FOR GOD, AND GOD'S LOVE FOR US:

1. SAVING FAITH:
   b) Not all belief leads to salvation:
      1) *"You believe that God is one. You do well; **the demons also believe**, and shudder. But are you willing to recognize, you foolish fellow, **that faith without works is useless**?"* – James 2:19-20
   c) Legitimate faith leads to obedience:
      1) *"Through whom we have received grace and apostleship **to bring about the obedience of faith** among all the Gentiles for His name's sake."* – Romans 1:5

2. SAVING GRACE:
   a) Not all grace leads to salvation, nor does God's love imply salvation. God is gracious to all and loves all, yet many will reject His salvation:
      1) *"You have heard that it was said, 'YOU SHALL LOVE YOUR NEIGHBOR and hate your enemy.' "**But I say to you, love your enemies** and pray for those who persecute you, **so that you may be sons of your Father who is in heaven; for He causes His sun to rise on the evil and the good, and sends rain on the righteous and the unrighteous.** "For if you love those who love you, what reward do you have? Do not even the tax collectors do the same? "If you greet only your brothers, what more are you doing than others? Do not even the Gentiles do the same? "**Therefore you are to be perfect, as your heavenly Father is perfect**."* – Matthew 5:43-48

2) *"For God so loved the world, that He gave His only begotten Son, that **whoever believes in Him shall not perish**, but have eternal life." – John 3:16*

b) Faith and repentance are required for saving grace:

1) *"And **that repentance for forgiveness of sins would be proclaimed in His name to all the nations**, beginning from Jerusalem." – Luke 24:47*

2) *"And saying, "The time is fulfilled, and the kingdom of God is at hand; repent and believe in the gospel." – Mark 1:15*

3. Knowing God:

A. Talking to God in prayer does not necessarily mean we know God:

1) *"If anyone turns a deaf ear to my instruction, even their prayers are detestable." – Proverbs 28:9*

2) *"Many will say to Me on that day, 'Lord, Lord, did we not prophesy in Your name, and in Your name cast out demons, and in Your name perform many miracles?' "And then I will declare to them, '**I never knew you; DEPART FROM ME**, YOU WHO PRACTICE LAWLESSNESS.'" – Matthew 7:22-23*

3) *"If we say that **we have fellowship with Him** and yet walk in the darkness, we lie and do not practice the truth." – 1 John 1:6*

4) *"The one who says, **"I have come to know Him,"** and does not keep His commandments, is a liar, and the truth is not in him." – 1 John 2:4*

B. Knowing God means being in a covenant relationship with Him:

   1) *"For I delight in loyalty (covenant love) rather than sacrifice, And in the knowledge of God rather than burnt offerings." – Hosea 6:6 (emphasis added)*

   2) *"**For this reason He is the mediator of a new covenant**, so that, since a death has taken place for the redemption of the transgressions that were committed under the first covenant, those who have been called may receive the promise of the eternal inheritance." – Hebrews 9:15*

C. If we say we love God we will strive to obey Him:

   1) *"**For this is the love of God, that we keep His commandments**; and His commandments are not burdensome." – 1 John 5:3*

   2) *"If you love Me, you will keep My commandments." – John 14:15*

4. Scripture teaches us to examine ourselves to see if we are of the faith:

   a) *"**Test yourselves to see if you are in the faith; examine yourselves**! Or do you not recognize this about yourselves, that Jesus Christ is in you-- **unless indeed you fail the test**?" – 2 Corinthians 13:5*

   b) *"**But a man must examine himself**, and in so doing he is to eat of the bread and drink of the cup." – 1 Corinthians 11:28*

c)  *"For there must also be factions among you, so that those who are approved may become evident among you." – 1 Corinthians 11:19*

**Are we ready for the end time revival?** The wheat and the tares are growing at the same time, and the bride of Christ cannot look to the tares for their model. The wise, burning bride will be looking at Christ and His word; having His word hid in their hearts. The great apostasy and the great revival.

It is imperative that the church be rooted and grounded in God's word, because the time is coming when everything will be tested by fire. Everything that can be shaken will indeed be shaken, and the only ones who will stand will be those who are founded on the Word of the Lord. The preservation of the Gospel and sustained revival go hand in hand. It is time for the proclaimer to stand and not budge on God's definitions of love, pure grace, saving faith, and true repentance. While love, loves truth, wisdom is full of mercy and both are necessary.

JOSHUA ALVAREZ (B. S. Southwestern Assembly of God University) is associate pastor at Unshackled Church in Pasadena, TX. Contact: joshuaalvarezbook@gmail.com

Notes:

Notes:

Notes:

Notes:

Notes:

Notes:

Notes:

Notes:

www.ingramcontent.com/pod-product-compliance
Lightning Source LLC
LaVergne TN
LVHW051604080426

835510LV00020B/3122